"Trust in the Lord with all your heart, and lean not on your own understanding; in all your ways acknowledge Him, and He shall direct your paths."

(Proverbs 3:5-6 NKJV)

SETTING A
TRUE COURSE

"God made life simple.

It's man who complicates it."

C. Lindbergh
72

SETTING A
TRUE COURSE

Flight Plans for Life

Gerry R. Wevodau

ACKNOWLEDGEMENTS

Everyone has someone—or many—to thank for their success or their inspiration in life. (You know those Academy Award-type of "Thank-Yous" that NEVER seem to end?)

First, my faith in a Living God and His Word is my utmost inspiration, but He uses others to do His work, too.

My wonderful wife, Yvette, inspires me every day with strength to go on, no matter what; my kids and my siblings inspire me, too.

I have a wonderful friend I get to see almost every work day, Connie Caka, who has termed herself "the work wife." We have a wonderful friendship that only comes along once in a lifetime for some; she is a confidant and trusted adviser who helps me keep in balance professionally.

My business partner and daughter, Emily, is also one of those who is comfortable enough to speak her mind and give valuable input when necessary.

Sara, another co-worker whom I mention in a chapter, is a valuable asset to our growing team here in our business.

Jim Douglas, my "brother from another mother," has taught me much about spiritual things; he and other friends are mentioned here in this book.

Also, I want to give credit to my friend "Tremendous" Tracey Jones, who helped me compile this writing into a format that hopefully encourages you.

I could go on and on, but I wanted to mention some of those who are close and in my "tribe." It would be too long of a list to include everyone, so don't worry if you aren't mentioned by name. Those who are in my path in life and business know who they are. All of you encourage me!

TABLE OF CONTENTS

PREFACE

Just some quick notes as to what inspired me to write this book; it's just one of those "assignments" from above you will read about in the chapters ahead.

I'm a "*Simple Man*," like that old Lynard Skynard tune many of us grew up singing in our first car while listening to the 8-track player. (Millennials will have to Google what an 8-track player is—and possibly who Lynard Skynard is, for that matter! That's no dig on you personally; it's just part of a widening generation gap I'm becoming more aware of over time.)

This book is a simple approach to the "works" that we encounter in everyday life. A passage in Paul's letter to the Ephesians tells us we are saved by grace, not works, so we cannot boast about it. But it goes on to say in the preceding text that we are His workmanship, created for good works, which God prepared beforehand and we should walk in.

That's all this is—a strategy for others to "go and do likewise." This isn't deep theological writing, but a simple approach to life and my response to the opportunities to serve God by serving others. I'm just grateful for the opportunity to share a few experiences of life as I'm going through it. My hope is that it gives you a boost in life, a chance to dust yourself off and keep going, to be engaged in life, and to die with your boots on!

Gerry R. Wevodau

FOREWORD

When you get to work with someone on a book project, you get to understand them in the most authentic way possible. Gerry has been a staple in the "Tremendous" family for decades. He knew and loved my father and became a surrogate brother to me. I also was excited to learn more about Gerry and what made him so tremendous.

As a fellow aviation enthusiast, it was also insightful to hear Gerry weave the analogy of having flight plans for life. We can set the course, but when you go "wheels up," there's a tremendous amount of experiences that can happen in the wild, blue yonder. As we met month after month, his words were a blessed reminder that we need to go with the flow and let grace happen.

Gerry told me that the definition of a good landing is one you walk away from. A really good landing is one where they let you use the plane again. And when you're in "the soup," you've got to get above or below the clouds if you want to land on terra firma. His life experiences reflect these words and his humble attitude toward life.

Enjoy the insights from my tremendous friend. I know they will bless you as you chart your own true course in life. Be open, stay calm, and remember who you've got behind the control stick.

Tracey C. Jones
President
Tremendous Leadership

INTRODUCTION

Why am I writing this book? I was at an insurance event when my friend Paul Feldman put the seed of this project in my mind. I'm not a policy "wonk," nor would I bore the world with my professional insights. I consider this book an assignment from God, based on everyday, ordinary circumstances as well as divine events. I hope to share with, and prepare you for, what happens in real life; and I hope to encourage you.

Often the things you don't set out to do on purpose result in the biggest payoff. For instance, I didn't set out to become involved in prison ministry earlier in life, but in the process, the men's hunger to learn blessed me infinitely more than I probably impacted them. Life's like that.

When you're open to being used, you get handed some tremendous assignments. In a similar vein, I never pictured myself as an author, but as a father, husband, teacher, and businessman who graduated summa cum laude from the school of hard knocks. But here you are reading about my journey, and I am eternally grateful for that.

When you're a small business owner, you're out there floating on your own. Sure, you have employees, but leadership is lonely. You hope to have team members who will tell you what you need to hear, who are not overly optimistic but tell you like it is. Perhaps you're the kind of boss who doesn't like criticism or advice, but you need to hear it. It's all about having good accountability partners who come into your life in many different ways.

My hope is that the words in this book will be a lifeline for you in the sea of running your business. I want to put my arm around your shoulder, tell you how hard it is, and tell you some real-life stories of the things I've been through. Everybody has their pain, but it's encouraging to read about the struggles and challenges of others, and how they overcame them.

This gives us inspiration and encouragement. I did it, and so can you.

We all grow up with certain thought processes instilled in us by our family and surroundings. I was raised by a father who had a strong work ethic and the ability to harness the energy of three boys. He'd take us to his place of employment at a furniture store, where he'd put us to work cleaning, vacuuming, organizing, unloading trucks—you name it. I'm sure he was also giving my mother a welcome reprieve from three hellions. It was there that his work ethic was imprinted on me.

My parents were great role models, but life's instruction manual went like this: grow up, get a good job, take care of your family—and don't rock the boat. My father was not a risk taker. He had trepidation about stepping out and breaking new ground. As a result, so did I. A turning point came in my life, however, when I married at 17, became a father at 18, and worked at the same location as my father. I had to grow up very fast. I was on my second adult job when my father passed away in 1989, and I came to a crossroad. I didn't just want a J.O.B. the rest of my life, with somebody always telling me what to do; I wanted something more.

That's when I found the insurance world, and my fear of taking risks was put to the test. I learned how hard it was to survive on a commission, as well as how hard it was to get people to listen to you, let alone take action. As my mentor Charlie "Tremendous" Jones used to say, "When you're cold calling, put your head through the door and not your foot. That way when they close it, you can keep talking!" I had to learn a lot of critical skills through the hard knocks of life—how to think and how to speak. After thirty years of being forced to develop these skills, I grew in faith, in skill, in grit, and in persistence.

I learned that if you're a good listener, people will come to you. (There's a reason we have one mouth and two ears.) I also learned you must have something to give them, good and quick—otherwise, you're done for.

Insurance is the business of teaching people critical ways to manage life's risks. I feel most fulfilled when I can help others move forward by being patient, hands-on, and collaborative. I've seen a lot of heartache, and I give people the tools that can help get them through it. I spend the first one to two hours a day praying and pouring positivity into my head and heart so I can deal with the encounters of the day and help others.

Insurance isn't a job; it's an opportunity. It forces you to grow as a person. We deal with a lot of heartaches in the insurance industry, because we address some of the most critical issues of life—death, loss, you name it. When people hit a roadblock, I get the call. I am there to help them level the mountain in front of them or adjust their course to greener, more peaceful pastures, both professionally and personally. I'm the old warhorse that knows the pathways to get you there, because I've traveled them countless times. I hope you enjoy the ride.

Let me give one closing word on "Why a book?": whenever I went to Charlie "Tremendous" Jones for advice (or, God forbid, to suck my thumb), inevitably he'd whip a book off the shelf, thrust it into my hands, and direct me to read aloud. Halfway down the page I'd think, "What am I whining about?" Then we'd get down on our knees and pray, and he'd instruct me to talk to God.

I've seen the power of a book in healing a person's heartache—most of all, mine.

Piloting Your Plane

One of my passions is flying. When you get in the cockpit the first thing you do is set your CDI, or Course Direction Indicator. You turn the dial and set the arrow to the exact direction you want to go, with 360 degrees to choose from.

This is a brilliant metaphor for life. Knowing where you are going and setting the final destination is the first step in any goal-setting and vision-casting exercise.

How do you get off course in life? If you don't set the dial, you might land in enemy territory or wander into a no-fly zone. You'll inevitably be blown off course by the winds of change, and sheered away by the trials of life. In life, we are constantly moving, realigning and making small course corrections; otherwise, we will end up far away from where we wanted or needed to land. I get tremendous satisfaction from being in the control tower of my client's life when they need it the most. I help them make those critical course corrections so they can fly high and land safely.

1

THE WAY THINGS WERE

I earned my badge of independence at a young age. As the youngest of three boys—all two years apart—I was frequently used as a punching bag. I couldn't fight back, so I did things on my own; this made me pretty self-reliant. My parents had their hands full when they took me to a store. I'd disappear, and they would have to spend their time trying to track me down. (My grandmother affectionately suggested they put a leash on me so I wouldn't run off.)

My father was larger than life and an exceptional salesman, the kind of guy who could talk to anybody.

I learned my love for people and conversation from him; everybody liked him, and he was a genuine guy.

It was a simpler time. Our family would go for drives, just spending time together in the car and enjoying the open road. I spent a lot of time around adults and learned a great deal about life. I remember going on trips to Philadelphia with some of my dad's sales team in the furniture business. We went to Veterans Stadium and had fancy dinners at the legendary restaurant Bookbinders. I learned how to shake a man's hand with meaning—and not like a dead fish!

I have many great memories from those experiences with my father. To this day my brothers and I reminisce about them. In the early years of my adulthood, I had the pleasure to work with my dad and learned so much from him about what it means to be a man. We worked together for the last three years of his life, before his sudden death from a massive heart attack at the age of 48. That's too young to die, but life isn't in our hands; Scripture tells us our days are ordained (Psalm 139:16).

It was time for a change after my father passed. Two months later I responded to a help-wanted ad for insurance sales. They say success is inspiration and perspiration, but in the beginning what drove me was desperation and exasperation. But it was all good. I no longer worked for someone else, I worked for me. I was master of my destiny. The harder I worked the more successful I became. It wasn't perfect or ideal, but it did meet the goal of supporting my wife, two children, and soon to be third child on the way—that's desperation man! My wife wouldn't let me in the door without any applications and checks! Desperation can sure make you successful—failure is NOT an option.

My grandparents were products of the depression era, people who worked in factories and bakeries. My father saw that and got into furniture sales in the late 1950's and climbed into management. He was very successful at dealing with people. In that era, people did what they did based on the recommendations, connections, and advice of other people. I observed how they operated and took it all in.

They say you're a product of who you surround yourself with. I watched as my father worked well into the night at the furniture store, with a goal to become top salesman or even the manager of the operation. As a young boy, all I wanted to do was to wait up and see my dad come home, tell him about my day and share a story. I said to myself, "When I grow up I am not going to have to work late."

I often could not stay up long enough and would fall asleep on the couch. I guess from the beginning I was an early-to-bed and early-to-rise person. To this day I wander off to bed by 9:30 every night while my wife can stay up past 11 p.m. if she isn't working the next day. I guess "opposites" do attract, in more ways than one. Because of this, I decided to become a businessman because businessmen have meetings with business people during the business day. In other words, no late nights away from home! That was a great way to get to see my family grow up. I did work some evenings, but not more than one to two a week in the beginning, and now I rarely do.

You can do anything you put your mind to. Even though my early foray into the world of work alongside my father wasn't ideal, or conducive to entrepreneurship, I realized that sometimes we know what we have by what we don't have. That's true of life as well. I made observations about what I liked and what I didn't want to be subject to. That early memory of the way things were growing up gave me the impetus to not be out at night, and if I had to, only on a limited basis.

One great memory I have (once we had our own family) is when my wife wanted the kids to go to a private Christian school. I thought, "I went to public school, and I turned out alright." So I challenged her: if she wanted to do that, she could figure out how to pay for it. So she did. My wife is so competitive, anytime I challenge her she rises to the occasion; that's one of the many things I admire about her.

She decided to get into home party sales, selling Tupperware® about four to five evenings a month. This gave me the opportunity to take care of the kids after working all day; looking back, those were fun times. After dinner we would play games, read books or watch a video; maybe a bath and then off to bed. Man, was I exhausted!

Those experiences made me appreciate what she did all day to keep three energetic kids occupied— and out of juvenile hall! She still, to this day, can run circles around me with her energy and enthusiasm for life. She is an inspiring personality. I love that cute girl I married thirty-four years ago and will never stop loving her, no matter what.

2

The Things I Thought Were Important

Many people in our great country have misconceptions about what success is. America is a land of great opportunities. But success isn't about making money or having financial independence. People with money have a saying: "Money doesn't buy you happiness, but it sure makes the misery more bearable." Sure, you need to be independent enough to pay the bills and take care of your family. But beyond that success is not a level of income. Once you meet your obligations, it becomes so much more than that. Success is your level of serving others, the bonds of familial love, the quest of following your purpose, the people in your life, your friends and family.

My old friend Charlie Jones used to say, "You'll be the same five years from now except for two things—the *people* you meet and the *books* you read." This is very true. The books you read give you a perspective on life—maybe a new and fresh perspective when you are in a desert land searching for answers. People can be good or bad, but we can always learn from them.

I've met some wonderful people in my everyday life in the insurance business, who inspire and encourage others by their strength to overcome. I've met some terrible ones, too, who only attempt to tear others down. (Maybe they want to tear others down to their level because they want company down there, I don't know.)

Never let negative people tear you down to their level—rise up and be encouraging. I heard a saying once: "You catch more bees with honey than vinegar." I like that saying—it's a truism. Another simple truth to live by is what we know as the "Golden Rule"—do to others as you'd have them do to you. Regardless of your faith or beliefs, this is just a great way to live.

Inherently, we all want to make more money. Money is a wonderful tool, but a terrible master— and you can be mastered by money, whether you have a lot or a little. People without a lot of money think having more will make everything easier for them— and the worst part of that lie is, it's partly true! Money doesn't make you happier, but it does give you more opportunities.

The fact is, the importance we place on money in our lives defines our happiness and success. Your health is more important than money. Relationships and friendships, having people who love you, is more important, whether it's familial love or your tribe— the people you rub shoulders with every week, the influencers in your life.

You need the right people around you to encourage you. While you have your own challenges and struggles, we are all in this life together. It's best to have people near you who are positive and encouraging—and to be that kind of person yourself. That's why, when my business colleagues and I bring people into the business, we make sure that their values coincide with ours; otherwise, we have problems. Remember, "misery loves company." Don't invite this in—life is hard enough on its own.

Insurance is no different—it can be a great thing when you need it, but it sure is painful paying those premiums when you don't! People have to think openly about the future and how they can spend their money to prepare for it. But some people don't want to think about the future at all, let alone what to do about it today.

People who love their families buy life insurance. It's the last real love letter you leave for them. It's far easier to just kick the can down the road, pretending you're going to live forever. The money won't bring you back, but if you're not there, the money will be there in your stead to meet their needs. It will bring peace of mind because they won't have to struggle to survive. It will mean less worry for your spouse, by solving the problems of a single parent: how to get by on one income, how to educate the children, how to afford to stay in the home they made with you. It's incredible how just a small premium can provide tremendous security for your family, the most important people in your life!

Everyone reading this book will at some point no longer be present with us. I've lost many friends and family members over the years; I'm sure you have as well. You need a plan to continue to meet the needs of those who depend on you, even after you're no longer around. My father didn't have a big policy and we watched how that failure to plan well financially left my mother and the rest of us hurting. She had to go back to work, with my little sister still at home. That impacted me on the importance of being well insured.

It was not an easy time in life, but we made it through. My mother is incredibly strong and tough when she needs to be. We used to joke that she had "hands like Joe Frazier" when she'd come after us kids. Tough but loving, she did a great job supporting our family.

People who don't have a lot of money think that having more will bring them happiness, when it may bring just the opposite. I know more wealthy people who are miserable than you might believe. It's the love of money, and where we place it, that determines if it's your servant or your master. I love and appreciate the life insurance business and what it means to those left behind. Proper life insurance protection can be your legacy. Make sure it's a good one.

3

The Seasons of Life: Good versus Bad

My grandparents had a great impact on my life. My father was an only child, and his mother exerted a tremendous spiritual influence on the family; it was my grandmother who took us to church. She loved us through a whole spectrum of life events. You may know this type of person—she showed us unconditional love, no matter what. She used to say, "Gerry Richard, you'll never change—and that's what I love about you!" Having her in my life was a joy and losing her was a great sorrow.

I went on to have three great children, all of whom left home in the span of a month; it was hard to go from a family of five to two. My oldest son is an emergency nurse for Kaiser Health System in southern California. He was always such a good kid and a people pleaser. He was unique and gifted in a lot of ways—always smart and very content.

I'll never forget the time when, as a growing boy of 12 or 13, he thought it would be fun to jump on his sister's antique bed—a family heirloom which brings to mind some great memories, and to which we were emotionally attached (maybe a little too much).

Well, you can guess what happened. Fortunately, I was outside cutting the grass and missed the crashing noise and the resulting the drama in the house. It broke his heart to have to come outside (on his mother's orders) and tell his 6' 4", 230 lb. father—who probably scared him to death—what he had just done.

Ever have something like that to deal with? When he came outside, I shut off the mower and watched him convulse with tears as he told me what happened. I was glad I had time to think about my ultimate reaction. There was a time when I would have exploded, but I realized he was more afraid of my reaction than anything else. I took a deep breath and told him to go inside and we'd talk about it when I was finished mowing the lawn.

I'm glad I handled it that way; I had time to think about it and come up with a teachable moment. We decided the drama was enough emotional turmoil for one day, and we made arrangements to get the bed repaired properly by an antique restoration specialist. Then I told him, "Guess what? You're going to pay for it!" That summer he had to do all kinds of jobs for us, the neighbors, and his extended family to pay the repair bill. Lesson learned, by him and me. I was proud of him—and myself, for not losing it!

My daughter was an honor roll student and like my oldest, she never did anything wrong (ha!). You know that's not really true, but when she's "Daddy's girl," sometimes that's how it seems. When she was bad, she was so smart about her deviant behavior that it was like a covert operation—I hardly knew it.

The toughest thing I had to deal with was when she decided to declare her independence by moving out. (You dads out there—and you moms, too— know what I'm talking about.) When she needed help moving back in after six or eight months because she missed home, I didn't hesitate.

When she sold me on her new husband, I realized how skilled she was in the power of persuasion. I was so impressed by her smarts and talent (greater than mine!) that I had to hire her on full time in the business. I made her a partner, because I could see a better future with her around for the long run. Best decision I ever made!

My youngest was a challenge to raise—more for me than his mother. His middle name, Nathan, meant "Gift of God" in Hebrew, but he was not what I expected. When he was three, he was quite a terror to his eight-year-old brother, chasing him around the house and grabbing the nearest thing he could find to hit him with.

But he was the cutest kid. Everybody just thought he was adorable—and that was the problem. He got away with far more than he should have, and it was my job to nip that in the bud. I was a John Wayne-type dad, trying to deal with a "rebel without a cause" son, and needless to say, we clashed. Trouble in school and life just followed him—I cannot imagine why! (That is a joke.)

He didn't want to go to college; he wanted to join the U.S. Navy. When I asked why, he replied, "Because I wanna travel the world and party!" I said, "Yes, you should join the Navy" (not because I thought that was a good reason, but because I hoped the Navy would teach him some discipline and direction). So he signed up. I cried at his boot camp graduation. My heart swelled with pride when he was voted platoon leader by his peers and Chief. I thought, "Finally he's on a good path serving our country."

His problems never went away, however; they followed him. When things went wrong, it was never his problem. Then he ran afoul of the law, and was incarcerated— that was a game changer.

So there I was, going back to prison—not to lead Bible studies as I had previously, but to visit my own flesh and blood. People complain about how hard prison is, and it is. That's because the system isn't designed to be your friend. It's designed to get your attention in such a way that you never, ever want to wind up on the inside again. Such was the case with my son, who served three years behind bars. It's what had to happen to get my child to where he needed to be. Even the bad seasons are there for a reason.

The good news is, my son was rescued, because when he was physically arrested, he was spiritually arrested as well. He broke out of his defiant attitude and grew as a man. He is now involved with his local church and living with his brother and our grandson. He has turned the bad into good. Looking back on this experience, I didn't like going through it; it was excruciating for me and my wife. If I'd been given the choice to avoid it, I would have. But it's what had to happen—it was God's direction in our lives. We had to accept it and stick together, no matter what!

There's the Lord's will, God's providence, and then there are our choices. All of these things flow in and out of the seasons of life and determine which are joyful and which are sorrowful.

But I learned that within every bad choice is a seed of redemption. My son was an attention seeker and needed a spiritual slap in the face. God's providence allowed it to happen—mercifully and graciously. The most tragic things of life always have the seeds of redemption in them; if we let them, they will cause us to grow.

When my co-worker's mother retired, we helped her with retirement health benefits. Unfortunately, she was diagnosed with breast cancer not long after that, and the side effects of the treatment temporarily limited her mobility. This hit my co-worker very hard in many ways, because she and her mother are quite close.

One day I got on my motorcycle and went for a ride to clear my head. I stopped at my favorite little country diner. Since my coworker is also a fan of this diner, I texted her to ask if she'd like anything brought back to the offices. More sarcastically than anything else, she joked in her responding text that maybe I should take her mom dinner, since she lived so close to the diner.

I took that as an opportunity to be on "assignment" and do just that. After some prodding from me, my coworker agreed to let me help.

So here I was, with two dinners—one for her mother and one for her hard-working step-father, a dairy farmer. The only problem was, I didn't know exactly where they lived, and I'd forgotten to ask my coworker!

I shared my challenge with the gentleman sitting next to me at the counter. He asked who they were, and I admitted that I only knew their first names and that he was a dairy farmer (I hadn't planned this very well, obviously!).

"Well, I know them—they are great people!" he responded. "I'll show you where they live."

It's funny how that all worked out. I stopped by her mother's house, made a new friend, encouraged her for a few minutes, said a prayer, and was on my way. It didn't take long, not much of my day, and I think I was more blessed than she was.

That was my assignment for the day. I didn't set out to do it, but I got handed an assignment along the highway of life.

The things we go through are for a reason. We go through heartache so we can have the empathy to encourage others. What kind of assignments do you have set before you? I encourage you to be open to what comes your way; you will be blessed when you respond in a good way!

4

FINDING OUT
WHAT MATTERS

We all grow up with a preconceived idea of the way life is. I fell in love at a very early age. Thank God we're still married today, by His grace and because I have a great wife. I probably wouldn't even be married if it wasn't for her. I have to give her a lot of credit, along with God's goodness. I was very young, literally a month away from being 18, when we got married.

I became a dad at 18, and then life hit me between the eyes. I said to myself, "Yikes! I'm responsible for other people's lives, not just my own. I can't be a kid anymore!"

I had to grow up fast, and I relied a lot on advice from my father. He was an excellent guide. All of us grew up going to him as the "answer guy." We even actually worked together. I had the privilege of working with him for the last three years of his life at Fry Communications, where we sold advertising for *The Guide* newspaper in the mid-1980s. When he suddenly passed away, I thought to myself, "Man, you've got to get out of here." That's when I embarked on my journey in the insurance business. When you get into in the insurance world, it's hard. You have to go out and do things you are very uncomfortable doing—calling people, face-to-face conversations, presenting. Your whole livelihood is based on whether you are skilled enough to convince them to buy what you have.

The company I started had a one-call close technique. In other words, you're either going to sell them a policy, or you're walking away. There's no "Would you like to think about it?" You had better make it a good first call. It was cold calling at its purest, and straight commission—no base salary.

The pressure to succeed was even greater because I had a wife and two kids at home. Then, right after I got into the business, my wife learned she was pregnant with number three! I found out about it by accident. When a friend called and asked for Yvette, I said, "Yeah, hold on a second." I called for Yvette to pick up the extension, but before I had a chance to hang up I overheard her say, "Did you tell Gerry?" I hung up the phone, turned ashen gray, and said to myself, "Oh, no, she's pregnant." And sure enough, she was! She had been too afraid to tell me, but when she did, I couldn't stop laughing! That was how I got in this business, and why I had such pressure to perform—#3 was on the way, and failure was not an option!

It was right after Thanksgiving of 1989 when I started in the business, the time of year when people's budgets are exceptionally tight with holiday expenses, and buying insurance is the last thing on their minds. By 1990, I realized I had to grow up quickly and learn on my feet to make a living. By 1992, when I met Charlie "Tremendous" Jones, I was doing pretty good—or so I thought. I had even been sent on incentive trips given by the company to those who met certain production requirements. This was not just any old trip, but a really nice one, to exotic places; I even stayed at a Ritz-Carlton. The first time

I ever rode in a plane was on one of these trips, when I was about 24 years old. (Now I fly airplanes for fun.) Those trips made a permanent impression on me.

I got to fly, and go to a lot of beautiful places—Jamaica, Montreal, Hawaii, and other great trips. I thought, "Wow, this business isn't that bad, if you persevere and hang in there!" It's interesting, my dad had this little two-word saying above his desk, which I have in my office to this day, Calvin Coolidge: "Press on." The full quote says,

> *"Nothing in this world can take the place of persistence. Talent will not; nothing is more common than unsuccessful men with talent. Genius will not; unrewarded genius is almost a proverb. Education will not; the world is full of educated derelicts. Persistence and determination alone are omnipotent. The slogan: 'Press On!' has solved and always will solve the problems of the human race."*

I hung onto that, and I still have it to this day. It's stuff like this that would get me going. I would think to myself, "Well, sitting here feeling sorry for yourself isn't going to get anything done." I knew that getting down and discouraged wasn't going to fix anything, so I had to realize what mattered: I had to take care of my family. They were my first responsibility, and quite frankly, without my relationship with God, I don't know where I'd be because He was my biggest motivator.

I also have to give my wife a lot of credit; she was a great supporter and a great cheerleader. She would give me these little boosts of encouragement. I'd come home all down, with my head hanging, and she had this little cheer she learned in school that she still does today:

> *You can do it, put your mind to it,*
> *buckle down, buckle down,*
> *do it, do it, do it!*

As she said this, loudly and with great enthusiasm, she would put her hands on opposite knees, then up to her hips, then her shoulders, ending with her arms up in the air, wearing the biggest grin. When she would do that, I would just crack up laughing. I thought, "Oh my God, how can I be down when she's standing there literally cheering for me?"

There were times when I would get discouraged, and I'm sure she didn't want to hear it, but she didn't pity me; she just gave me a swift kick in the pants. She never said, "Oh, I'm so sorry, honey," or those kind of things. Her response was more like, "Well, you don't have an option. You've got to get to work!" She was a stay-at-home mom for twenty years, and we had a family to support. I wasn't supposed to be staying at home. She was the one at home; I was supposed to be getting out there. So, I got out there and hustled!

Those were my early years in the business, when it was beneficial to have not only the support of a wife, but a friendship with Charlie Jones. He was such an encouragement! He didn't let anybody come and suck their thumb. When you came to visit him, he'd make you read passages from a book, and then say, "Okay, now we're going to pray," and he'd just either grab your hand or get you down on your knees, right there in his office. "I want you to get down on your knees; we're going to talk to Jesus."

You'd sit there, looking for commiseration, and you'd never get it. He'd send you off, usually with a new book in your hand, and it was all good!

Then, in 1994, a friend of mine, Jim Bower, who had recruited me into the Gideons, wanted me to join his team and work at his agency as a contracted agent. He's another kind, godly man who taught me how to be a Christian in business, and not be ashamed of my beliefs. He taught me how to share my faith, to pray with people and for people—not in a harsh or abrasive manner, but in a kind and loving way—and to be genuinely concerned about them. He was a great mentor and a dear friend.

You probably have people like that, who cross your path throughout your life and leave an impact. I think we all have the ability to be that kind of person in someone else's life—if we're sensitive to that opportunity. After practicing this for almost 30 years, I'm becoming more sensitive to it now. It's all about timing.

A young salesman came into my office recently (one of my key staff people, who would typically intercept him, was on vacation), and I wound up interacting with him. I said, "I appreciate your hustle. I built my business on hustle like this." I think he appreciated getting some positive feedback; I'm sure he had plenty of doors slammed in his face.

I concluded the meeting by saying, "I'm probably not a great prospect for you right now because I'm locked up in a contract, but check back with me in a couple of years, maybe we can do something." Later I connected with him on LinkedIn, and said, "If you ever think about a career change, talk to me." The young man presented himself well, and apparently has been reasonably successful, since he's been doing the same job for seven years. That's an example of how we can be kind to others, instead of just blowing them off.

That's what happens when you start to realize what matters in life. We want to make money, and money is essential to pay the bills. It's a tremendous tool, but a terrible master. I said before, friends who have money say, "Money doesn't buy you happiness, but it sure makes the misery more bearable." I'd rather have it than not, but it's not everything. When we leave this earth, we don't take any of it with us.

In life as well as business, it takes a while to learn that it's not really about money, but about your freedom, your time, and your work/life balance. Money does give you some freedom of time, but I think what we do with our time is just as important as what we do with our money. In the end, that's what matters.

5

Those Who Point You in the Right Direction

Two types of people are critical to your success in life: those who orient you where you need to go, and those with the power of observation to see where you've been.

The power of observation is another way of saying someone is sensitive. People may say, "I'm not very sensitive," but they are observant. We can learn a great deal by observing those who point us in the right direction. I think observant is the right word because God gave you one mouth and two ears for a reason. You're supposed to listen twice as much as you speak.

If you ask the right leading questions, it's interesting how you can get people to talk to you about almost anything and open their hearts to you. But there is a difference between sharing your heart and having a teachable heart.

I had a conversation with a friend the other day who shared some very personal things with me about his family. But he's one of those guys who is very subjective in his thought process. By that I mean he had the attitude that "this is the way I think things should be; I don't care what anyone else thinks."

We got into a discussion about things in the Bible, and if it didn't jive with his way of thinking his response was, "I don't believe that to be true." He was rigid, not able to unlearn and relearn.

When I was growing up, I used to watch reruns of the TV show *Dragnet*. The star of the show was a guy named Sergeant Friday, who was the soul of objectivity. He used to say, "Just give me the facts, ma'am." I try to be objective in my approach to business and to life, and I try to be open to both sides of the equation.

That's not the political climate we see today. This country is so divided it breaks your heart. Things that matter to all of us—freedom, the military, "In God We Trust," and family—should unite us, not divide us.

I collect coins, and one of my favorites is the Morgan Silver Dollar. On this coin is a Latin phrase, our country's original motto: *E Pluribus Unum.* Adopted in 1782, it means "out of many, one" or "one from many." It reflected our heritage of diversity, tolerance and respect for one another. This is something we need to be reminded of today, especially in Washington.

That's what I mean by being too closed, too subjective in your thought process. But there are people who can teach you how to be teachable. I had a friend who mentored and trained me to disciple others in the faith. I realized, after learning from him, that I had the gift of teaching. Even though I didn't want to do it, it was one of the assignments that God had for me in life. I expressed this gift by doing prison ministry, and teaching in the prisons.

Because of the terrible suffering caused by criminals in our nation, many people refuse to hear the viewpoint of prisoners, or even give them the time of day. I would often say to the inmates, "I didn't want to come here tonight, but God dragged me in here, and my heel marks are out on the front sidewalk." I was so blessed by them—when I got there, they were hungry to learn, they asked outstanding questions and they were engaged. They were open to learn and explore new truths. When I left there, I was more blessed than they were because it felt like I was being used in a compelling way to deliver a good message. I was encouraged; even if I went in with my head hanging down, I always left with my head up.

In teaching, there's a term we call F.A.T.—Faithful, Available, and Trainable. If you can be faithful to what God has for you, and make yourself available with your time, and be trainable to learn something new, you can be used. It's interesting how those experiences set me up for some of the personal experiences I've shared before—like our son being incarcerated. If I hadn't been familiar with "the system" by going into prisons, I would have been very intimidated by it. By the time that happened in my life, twenty years later, it was no big deal.

The people in your life who help you are your mentors. I've mentioned Jim Bower before. Like Charlie "Tremendous" Jones, he was a great mentor to me in how to be a good and godly businessman. Charlie Jones used humor so intelligently, to connect with people. He taught me how to be enthusiastic, love God's word, and how to laugh at myself. His talks were always hilarious, but they always made a point.

I think back on another theme of his: motivating the motivator. What do you do when your motivator is so discouraged that he can't get motivated anymore? It's really up to you. I always say, look at the man in the mirror—he's the one who's going to tell you to do it. This is where we have to get our motivation. It comes from within, whether it's asking God for strength, or reading books—and I'm a big believer in both.

I love to read every day—something new and fresh, and then something familiar. It has to be something I can identify with that is inspiring or encouraging. This is all part of being open and teachable, because life, as you know it, is a learning experience that never ends. We need to keep learning until the day we walk off of this earth.

I think it's exciting to get up every day, put your feet on the floor, and go out with the attitude, "What am I going to learn today?" Sometimes, though, we don't want to live what we've learned. Sometimes we read to unlearn. We read to unlearn those messages in our minds that are not fruitful, not encouraging, not good for our souls. Your soul is who you are as a person, your mind, will, and emotions. It's what makes you...you. It's what makes each of us unique. We need to read to unlearn the negative, discouraging messages from our enemy, who wants to intimidate us.

It's vital that we have a good message for people—words that encourage and lift up. Even in the times when we have to be very honest and not just fluff somebody up, telling them what they want to hear. One of the mottoes I learned from Jim Bower was, "We tell you the truth, whether you want to hear it or not."

I try to live that motto, but there's a right way to deliver it. A young man came to our office for an interview, and I was very blunt with him. I said, "It's up to you if you want to succeed, but I have to tell you that your appearance, mannerisms, and actions will not make you successful in our world." I outlined for him what he would have to do, and I gave him a copy of Charlie and Tracey Jones' book, *Message to Millennials* (Tremendous Leadership, 2017). "Read this and come back to me with a report on what this book means to you," I said. "If you come back with that, and you come dressed properly for a meeting, we'll have a discussion."

I had to tell him that, kind of give him a "love slap," like in the old Aqua Velva TV commercial from the 70s, where a man gets a slap in the face and says, "Thanks, I needed that."

Sometimes you need to give someone a loving slap, but you need to do it in a caring way—not disrespectfully, not to hurt their feelings, because being direct can come across as being mean. I'm never mean-spirited in my approach, just direct and transparent—transparent as in, "I'm not hiding anything from you; this is where the deficiencies are. This isn't my opinion; this is life. If you don't get your act together, life is going to be tough." I'm no expert at it, but I'm learning that this approach, when done tactfully, has been helpful. We never stop learning, *if* we are open to growing from our experiences. Be open to learn, or even *un*learn, today—your future success may depend on it!

6

Going through the Trials of Life

When you go through trials, and we all do, we have misery. There are those of us old enough to remember that old show called *Hee Haw*. They used to sit on the front porch, and sing that song with a country twang, "Misery, oh misery, oh woe is me, such misery." Those are the kinds of shows I grew up watching at my grandparent's house, that, and *Lawrence Welk*.

Some people teach you things in life without even knowing it. My grandparents are a good example.

They were beautiful people, born a hundred years ago, and they lived through the Great Depression, World War II and the Industrial Revolution. They were married in the mid-1930s and had my father in 1941. They were hard-working, salt-of-the-earth people, great neighbors and good friends. They had people in their lives that I thought were relatives, because my grandparents were such good friends to them, and would do anything for them.

My grandmother wanted more children, but couldn't have them (medical advances weren't what they are today), so she treated us kids like her own. Like any good grandparents, they spoiled us, and loved us. My grandmother was a person of strong faith. She taught the first Sunday school class I went to, and was a good, godly person.

Even when my grandparents got into a spat (and I only remember maybe three of them in my whole life), they would forgive each other quickly and move on. He used to call her "Toots," and next thing you know, he'd have his arms around her, and they'd be hugging and kissing and making up. It was a great lesson in forgiveness for all of us!

Those are the little things in life that you remember—if you argue with your spouse, ask forgiveness and move on. You don't hold on to the anger and unforgiveness. The Bible says, "Be angry, and sin not." It's okay to get angry and disagree, but then you have to get over it.

We all know people who become bitter and angry, and don't know how to let go of the past. They pride themselves on never forgetting when someone has wronged them. This wrong attitude makes you a prisoner of your own unforgiveness. It's well said that unforgiveness is like drinking bitter poison, and expecting the other person to get sick. You're not hurting them by not forgiving. You're only destroying yourself from the inside.

I don't think my grandparents, or even some of my mentors like Jim Bower and Charlie Jones, got up every morning and said to themselves, "What new thing am I going to teach to someone today?" They just made themselves available and taught us something along the way.

My wife taught me things by not taking me so seriously. I tend to be too much of a thinker, buried too deep into my own thoughts at times. But there are times when you shouldn't think so deeply, and my wife reminds me of that. At 54 years old, she still has a refreshing, child-like viewpoint to life—the "It's a Small World" ride at Disney World is still one of her favorites.

Having an unashamed, child-like faith has taught me not to take myself so seriously all the time. When you take yourself too seriously, life is hard and you wind up being melancholy about life.

Life is hard enough on its own, you don't need to help it. You just have to learn how to overcome it, to play the hand you've been dealt.

I saw this report the other day, of a young man on the news. While he was serving our country in the Marine Corp, he stepped on an IED, lost both his legs, and was blinded. After he went through rehab and recuperated, he reenlisted, because he wanted to continue to serve the nation he loves. He's now retired after completing two tours and eight years in the military.

That guy inspires me. What do I have to complain about? I can see, and I have both my legs. Why should I be down?

I see people in life that struggle physically, maybe due to a disability, or even a mental disability, but they're happy and smiling. These people encourage me. A friend of ours who goes to our church has some form of cerebral palsy. Her mind is perfectly fine, but she has difficulty walking. Yet she's always smiling, always happy, and always optimistic. I get so encouraged by her, and people like her. It makes you think, "What am I complaining about?" It's easy get discouraged by our circumstances, because we all have a preconceived idea of the way things should be. "I should be successful, I should have this, I should have that." We have to learn to be content with what we have.

Growing through the trials of life is a tie that binds because we all have trials. We all have temptations to do the wrong thing, and sometimes we give in to them; we make a left or a right when we should have stayed straight. I certainly can't say I've never made mistakes; I make mistakes too often to admit (and I'm not going to get into the nitty-gritty details), but we've all made mistakes in life. Some mistakes are more significant than others, but it doesn't matter. Whether it's something against the legal system or a sin against God, you have to learn from it and turn from it.

I'm thankful for the times I've been corrected by the Holy Spirit when I've done wrong. He has taken me to the woodshed, as I call it. In the most gentle and loving way, He's quietly said to my heart, "Son, that's not what you were created to do. That's not your role in life." It's hard to learn that, and when you're the boss, nobody wants to tell you when you're wrong. It's good to have people in your life that can say to you, "You're wrong."

Having the right tribe is essential. Your tribe—the people around you that can be honest with you, and not be afraid of repercussions—help you to be accountable in life. They speak truth to you in love.

First Corinthians 13 is called the love chapter. You can have all of these things in life, but if you don't have love, you've got nothing.

We all learn differently. Some of us learn from the mistakes of others, but many of us only learn from our own mistakes, from personal experience. I think we all have some of each kind of learner in us, but some may be more heavily weighted on the personal experience side. My son was one of those, because he thought he had it all figured out.

It may sound strange, but I'm *thankful* for the hardship my son endured—despite the fact that we went through years of heartache walking through it with him. I'm thankful first of all because he's still alive after all he's gone through, and secondly that my wife and I got to go through it with him.

When someone you love goes through something life-changing, you go through it too, whether you want to or not. Right at the beginning of his incarceration, I told him, "If you ever do anything like this again, all you'll see is the back of my head walking away. I'm not going to bail you out ever again. This is your opportunity to get your life squared away." I wasn't going to enable him to ever fail to that level again.

He had to hit bottom; he had to learn, "I'm not smarter than the law. I'm not smarter than my parents. I'm not smarter than my Chief in the Navy. I'm not as smart as I thought I was." What was so good is that God was with us through the whole thing. Because I am a pilot, we were able to get down there expeditiously, spend the day with him and fly home, all in one day. God provided for us through it all. The years he was incarcerated were very hard on both of us, financially, emotionally and spiritually. Everybody has those hard times in life, but we had hope and faith that we would get through it.

Sometimes you just can't do it on your own. You need faith in something bigger than yourself to help get you through. It is helpful to have friends who pray for you, encourage you and are just there for you, to be a listening ear when you're hurting and discouraged. I look at it this way: we're all in one big ship, sailing through life together. That's why I get so frustrated with the divisive politics in Washington D.C. I once read a book (I forget who wrote it) that said, "The D.C. in Washington means, 'Don't Care.'" They don't care about you; they're just going to do whatever they want to do. They have their own agenda.

The story of our son's incarceration was an example of growing through trials in life, and we all have many of them. Another hard trial for my wife and I happened about ten years ago. All our kids moved out of the house within a month's time, and we weren't expecting it.

Our oldest son moved out first, and we were expecting that; he came home from college and was working. It was time for him to leave the nest. "You don't need to be living at home," I said. "You need to figure out what you're doing and move on."

But then his sister moved out with him, to get away from the turmoil going on with our youngest son, who had just graduated from high school. As soon as the two oldest moved out together, our youngest one informed us that he was joining the Navy instead of going to college.

This sudden change was really hard on my wife and I; we went from a home of five down to just the two of us. We didn't know what to do with ourselves. Not just initially, but for a couple of years, we went through the pain and the heartache of wondering, "Where do we go from here? Are we going to spend the rest of our lives alone together?" My wife sought a lot of her relief through fellowshipping with friends. She is very creative and liked expressing herself through great artistic venues, such as scrapbooking and sewing quilts. She would have retreats on the weekends and get her fellowship fix, so to speak, by being around other women.

That left me alone to think, "Okay, what am I going to do now?" In the past when she was away on weekends, the kids would be home, and I would do things with them; but now they were gone, so it was just the dog and me.

That's when I started to re-evaluate what I should be doing with my life. We all go through these learning phases in life, whether due to a career change or just growing up. We all know someone who did something for twenty or thirty years, and suddenly got laid off. This happened frequently during the recession about ten years ago; a lot of people lost their jobs, and still haven't recovered into a solid career. They went from making a good living to scraping by on maybe two part-time jobs.

People go through phases in life, trials of all different kinds: losing a job, losing a loved one, physical and mental health issues, family issues, whatever. It's hard!

Losing a child has to be one of the most tragic things of all. I've known clients who lost children, whether in an accident, a drug overdose, or an illness; it was all very unexpected and very sad. No one ever plans to outlive their children. I saw it in my own family, because my dad passed away ten years before my grandmother, and it was hard on her.

We all go through trials, but take heart. Learn to look on the bright side. When you look outside, and all you see is a gray, cloudy day, remember that there's a sun above those dark clouds, and tomorrow's another day.

7

LEARNING TO BE
THANKFUL IN ALL THINGS

The most important thing about going through trials is to find joy in them. I know it sounds crazy, but the more we learn to be thankful in all things, the more content and joy-filled we will be.

It's interesting that while we all go through trials, when we get a reprieve, we tend to think, "Okay, I'm done with that. I'll never have to go through that again." I think we get little reprieves in life but then, inevitably, trials come along again, in some way. The key is to be thankful, in all things, no matter what.

There's always something good in every trial, even though we may not understand it. When one of my coworkers told me that her mom, who is dealing with cancer, had just finished her last radiation treatment, I said, "Man, it's a great day to celebrate. All I know is, life is hard, and it's never going to stop being hard." Yes, life is hard. But that's where faith, family, and friends come in—faith being the most important. A lot of it has to do with our attitude of thankfulness, and having the right mindset when we go through trials, because it's difficult to get encouraged by ourselves alone.

One of my favorite scriptures is Proverbs 3:5–6, where it says,

> *"Trust in the Lord with all of your heart, not with your own understanding, in all your ways acknowledge Him, and He will direct your path."*

Most of the time, when I write somebody a note, letter, or sympathy card, I always put that scripture on it, because I think we need to remind each other now and again to trust the Lord. "It's going to be okay. It's hard right now, what you're going through, but trust that it's going to get better." Lip service is the last thing I want to give somebody, but when I give an encouraging word, it comes from a heart of concern, and care for someone who has lived it and has a basic understanding of how hard life can be.

I try to put my arm around their shoulder and say, "Hey, I know it hurts really bad right now, but you're going to be okay, you're going to get through it if you trust God." We all need to be reminded that at times, instead of getting so discouraged that we want to give up. Some people get to that point of giving up because they have lost all hope, and that's a sad place to be.

When I first started in the insurance business, I was struggling. I had three little kids at home, I was on straight commission, and I needed money. All the money I earned was spent right away—I couldn't seem to earn it fast enough.

I learned, however, to start my day by thanking God—to just have a heart of thanks: "Lord, thanks for my health, that I can get up and go to work. Thanks that we have a house we can call home. Thanks for the support of a loving wife, and for three, healthy, beautiful kids who need me. Thank you for it all." By the time I got to the third or fourth thing I was thankful for, my heart was lifted, and I was not looking down. I was looking up, just being thankful.

Thankfulness is the key to happiness—or more accurately, to true joy. Happiness is a term we throw around too loosely. Happiness is circumstantial, based on external events: Did somebody treat you good today? Are good things happening in your life right now? Did you win the lottery? Do you have enough money? Happiness, in your own eyes, can only come from things going well for yourself, but when you're thankful, you can dig down deep and that's where joy comes in. There's a difference between joy and happiness. Happiness is based on your circumstances, but joy is a state of being content regardless of your present circumstances.

We need to be continuously reminded to control our thoughts and be grateful. I get a better perspective on my circumstances by reading stories in the magazine *Guideposts* about people dealing with big challenges in life—physical disease or danger, the loss of a loved one, a major career change—things much greater than my daily struggles. Little things like that just encouraged my heart.

I even gained a really great friendship from an article in *Guideposts*. Two years ago, I had hip replacement surgery, and I was taking those opiate medications that you hear so much about in the news. I read a *Guideposts* article about a man named Wayne Campbell, whose son Tyler had shoulder surgery as a collegiate athlete at the University of Akron. Tyler was taking opiates and became addicted—as one in four people can, because of their physical makeup.

These things are dangerous because they are chemically linked to heroin. There's a ninety percent or higher crossover in the chemical makeup of an opiate to heroin. Heroin, though, is much cheaper than opiates—a few dollars versus fifty to eighty dollars—and is more accessible on the street. Those who become addicted to opiates invariably go on to heroin. That's why we have such a drug problem in our country, because of treating people for post-surgical pain with these pills.

Wayne's son Tyler lost his life to this tragic epidemic, but the story doesn't end there. Encouraged by friends, Wayne turned his grief outward instead of inward and started an organization called Tyler's Light, a great education program where he presents the danger of this drug to kids in middle school and high school. He's been to a dozen states and spoken to about 180,000 kids since the program's inception. He has also created some award-winning videos on the subject.

When I read that article, it touched my heart so much that I sat there crying, thinking of all the trials my son had gone through and how thankful I was that he was still alive. I thought, "Here's a guy who went through as much or more than I did with my child, and he doesn't even have his son anymore." Overwhelmed by his story, and I reached out to him and asked what I could do to help. He said, "Well, you can keep telling the story, and if you want to sponsor me to come to your area and talk to the kids at the schools, I'll do that." So, in October of 2016, we did just that. He spoke to about eight thousand kids in the area and we are working to bring him back again.

8

DOING YOUR BEST TO ENCOURAGE OTHERS

Most days, we get so wrapped up in ourselves and our work that we forget about helping others. We need to stop focusing so much on "me, myself, and I" and focus outwardly. Look for connections with others and where they need to be made.

Someone once said to me, "When you finally get to the end of yourself, then the magic happens." We've got to be a vessel to be poured out, and God will do the refilling. I used to give that lip service but I never really lived it. I was at eighty percent, but God wants it all. He can't really help me shoulder this load until I'm prepared to say, "You know what, God? I don't need you for twenty percent of this, I need you to take it all." He wants nothing less than 100 percent—you just need to get out of your own way.

We all go through those growth experiences in our walk where we have faith and we trust God, but do we really give it all to him? You wind up holding onto little pieces of yourself, and that's where pride and self come in. It's also where you're going to run off the tracks.

I've done it in my own life, but I don't really want to share all those gory details. (Some mistakes you take to the grave with you; God knows them all and nobody else really needs to know.) When you screw up, it's because you take your eyes off one overarching fact: that your life—your business, your family, your everything—is not your own, it's God's.

My business is a ministry for people to encourage others, whether they're clients or team members, or whoever we get to interact with that day. Everyone is a part of it. This interconnectedness is so important because people are very unreachable today.

I am involved in a group for Christian business people called C12. The curriculum is highly interactive. You share challenges you are having, such as a problem with a client or employee, you get feedback from others, and it gets the mind working. Sure, there's a financial cost as well as a time commitment, but it can be invaluable because you build some good relationships. Ultimately, it's all part of the plan for your life, whether it's for the next six months or six years.

God has plans for each and every one of us. I have a friend who is incarcerated, and like most people in prison, it's because he did something stupid and foolish—acting more on impulse than reasoning. He's doing some time, more than he ever expected—a minimum of 5 years, and maybe more. He went from having his own business, serving people for 30 years, making a very good living, with a home and family—and he's lost it all. His family no longer talks to him because they were victims, too. He's lost his business because his actions impacted his employees; to avoid lawsuits, he's had to relinquish his rights to it.

He's right where God needs him to be to become whole—not just to make restitution to society, but to rescue himself. He had to come to the end of himself to be found and restart all over again.

He was a man of the church. You would think he had it all together. He was successful professionally and financially. He had it all—and all he had was stripped away from him.

I go to the prison to encourage him—and yet, I get encouraged. I learn so much from him—not just because of his life experiences but because while he's been in prison, he's been growing! He's playing the organ in the church choir and he's mentoring people inside. He's tutoring other prisoners because he's college educated and a professional—a physician by trade. He has a good mind and he's helping guys out who don't even have a high school education or a GED.

He realizes that it's all in God's hands and part of God's plan. He knows he'll be in prison not one day longer or one day less than he has to. It's all part of the plan, the plan we don't get to see.

It's the things we do that create these false things around us. God will put us into the wilderness because that's the only place where we can find intimacy with Him. He will break us in all the right places to make us stronger in Him.

I tell my friends I visit behind bars, "You will not be here one day longer than He needs you to be. If you're still here, there's still work that needs to be done in you and/or the people around you. Don't stress about parole because you will be out in God's time." And a lot of them admit that if they had gotten out earlier than they did, they would have been right back in.

Most often, truth doesn't come to us on its own. You need to have other people, other books, the Holy Spirit, speak into you because it's counter-intuitive when you're in the wilderness. It's one of those life paradoxes. Until you experience pain and heartache in life, you don't have a heart for others because you don't think it will ever happen to you.

Let me share a couple of stories with you of what I mean by this.

I've had several clients, unfortunately, pass away. One client friend came into my office in tears because he had just been told he had cancer—one of the hardest things for a person to hear—and was scared as to what was going to happen next. I had really grown close to this guy; I really appreciated him as a person. We had a lot of laughs together, a lot of good talks; we enjoyed working with him. I said, "Jim, I don't know what's ahead for you, but I do know God loves you. I'd like to pray for you if I can." He said, "That will be great." I went around the desk, put my hand on his shoulder, prayed for him and encouraged him, gave him a hug and said my final goodbye. Though he did pass away, I did what I could to try to lighten his load and be sincere, and not do it in an overbearing way. I wasn't pulling out the Bible and sharing the gospel, I was just trying to live it and love this guy and meet him where he was.

I recently had a meeting with another client who is also battling cancer. I was in a closed-door meeting with him and his wife and I asked him, "How are you doing, Wayne?"

"Not good."

"Do you mind if I pray for you?"

"No."

I did ask him, "Do you know Jesus as your Lord and Savior?" He said, "Yes, I do," and I replied, "Well, that's wonderful!" Then I just grabbed his hand and prayed for him and his wife.

Weeks later he called the office and said, "I really appreciate Gerry coming down and praying for me." I was there to talk to him about insurance as my job, but my assignment that day was to really encourage this guy.

The gentlemen in prison I mentioned earlier was all over the news. Twenty-five years ago, I would have been the guy complaining about how much it cost taxpayers to incarcerate someone. Then I got involved in a men's discipleship class where we ministered to those behind bars. Then our own son was incarcerated for three years. Pretty soon it gets to be the same thing, just somewhere else.

Society wants to throw these people away, but because of my interactions with them, I feel compassion for them. The group of men I taught were not like a typical Sunday school class where you could just get up and teach anything. These guys were studying the Bible all day long and asked some deep theological questions. I was blessed by their engagement. Here I was, coming to prison to encourage them, and these guys were encouraging me. That's a great life principle: the encourager always becomes encouraged.

It's amazing how this all happens. I fly out to Grove City repeatedly and the good news is, I get to do something that I'm passionate about, which is flying. It gives me a purpose to jump in the plane and take some brothers in the Lord out to make their day—and in the process, I get to fly!

It's funny how those little life experiences surface where you think you have your day planned, then you look at your calendar and there's a chance it may all happen, or that none of it happens, or that some of it happens. It's interesting how days unfold when you relinquish your life to God and it's not your day. It's His day, and He can use you.

When we hear the word, connecting, we think we must be busy bees; I have to go here, I have to network, I have to follow up, I have to be like Superman and make this many cold calls. That's the worldly way. Then there's the divine connecting, which is where you get out of your own way and let the Great Connector put you with those you need to connect with.

True connections happen in the inner landscape with intentionality. Something or someone is getting put on your heart or you read somebody's true needs, and you're not just making a sale or a commission. Somebody once told me, "We're coloring ourselves whole." In other words, I'm not just after you for what you can do for me, or for how you can grow my business financially. I'm pouring myself out in any way I can be of service to you, and that's at the heart of true authentic connection.

I was recently out with one of my team members, visiting a prospective client she had worked with five years ago at a previous agency. We made our presentation to him and met with him for a couple of hours, and had a nice meeting. We were twenty minutes away from another client who had an employee involved in a tragic industrial accident where a nineteen-year-old young man was killed.

One thing that we always do when people pass away is we send an "in memory" card and we buy Bibles from the Gideons for them. We had sent the Memorial Bible card to this young man's mother and family but we never sent one to the business. I told my team member to fill out another card so we could drop it by personally and give our condolences. We stopped in and gave it to them and said, "Hey, listen, we're praying for you guys and we know what's going on is really hard."

The wife of the owner of the business out came out around the corner with tears in her eyes because she heard what we were saying. We just gave her a hug and told her how sorry we were about their loss; it turned out the young man was a relative of the owner's family. We weren't there for more than ten or fifteen minutes, but it was another assignment that God had for us. It only took a half hour out of our day to drive the extra twenty minutes, pay our condolences, let them know we were praying for them, and be on our way. We didn't do it because we wanted to be liked, or because we expected to get something out of it. We did it because we care. People don't care how much you know until they know you care!

Everyone is afraid to talk to the boss, or to say something to someone in pain. I'm not afraid to talk to anybody. I'll talk to a homeless guy on the street. I'll talk to a prisoner in prison. I'll talk to the chairman of the board. They all put their pants on the same way; they're all people. From God's perspective, they're each an eternal soul and He loves them all.

God puts people on your heart like they're on his heart. That doesn't come naturally, that's divine. That's not from us, that's God.

When you fly a "Christ flight plan" for your life, even the turbulence may rattle your teeth, but He is in control of the "Final Destination." We may have to make an "emergency landing" from time to time and get on our knees to make things right, but we get back in the cockpit and finish the "flight plan."

9

Finding Joy in the Process

If you can't find joy in the process, there's no sense in going there. Happiness is just circumstantial and so many people are unhappy because their circumstances aren't perfect. If you're going to wait for perfect circumstances, you're never going to be truly happy. Joy comes in finding what your purpose is and doing it, no matter what the circumstances are, because they're never going to be perfect.

It used to frustrate me like crazy that I couldn't get accomplished what I set out to do in a day. But

I think I set out to do what I wanted to do, instead of what God had in mind. Have you ever had that happen to you?

I remember my mentor, Charlie "Tremendous" Jones, saying, "I'm so tired of being happy; it's wearing me out!" I always figured he felt that way because he's an optimistic, gregarious person, but now I get it. At the end of the day, when my head hits the pillow, I don't even know what day of the week it is. I have everything planned out, but every day, God sets the agenda; it's his assignment, it's not my day. I plan hard, I work hard, I sleep hard, and I'm so busy, I don't even know what year it is or how old I am. I am tired, but I am joyfully tired.

That's when you wind up finding joy in the changing circumstances of life rather than seeing it as drudgery. These assignments from God aren't simply something else to do that's tiring. It may be grueling, but it's godly. It's energizing because of the joy it brings. You finally stop fighting control of the yoke and rudder and let God be your pilot. I know what I have planned, but He orders the day. And that allows you to really dial in your flight plan. I use God pilot, not autopilot.

My plane has autopilot and it is very help-ful when you're a single pilot flying in instrument meteorological conditions, IMC. But the best way to get through difficult times in life is not autopilot, where you sit back and relax, but God pilot, where He takes care of it.

Allowing others to walk alongside us and help out also brings joy. We all need that kind of help, and if you don't have good people around you, it's hard. We've all had co-workers who were there just for a J.O.B. and others who really dig in and help; they stop by or email you on their day off—they're really committed. It always encourages me to know I have a team member I can rely on. I'm fortunate to have some team members like that, people you can count on in the trenches to get things done.

I recently visited a dear friend in a nursing home—Jim Bower, who, as I mentioned before, was one of my mentors. He had a stroke about a year and a half ago and can't really communicate well—his speech is very impeded and difficult to understand. I think he gets frustrated by that; he's communicated for a living, but is now trapped in his body, paralyzed on one side and dependent on others to take care of him. We come to encourage him, but I think we get encouraged by his wife and family and how they handle that challenge. It can be lonely in those kinds of environments, so we come to connect, to give and receive joy.

He was watching golf the day we stopped by because he used to play, so we talked about that and just hung out for a little while. Every time before we go, I grab his hand and his wife's hand, and pray with them, encourage them, and tell them that we love them.

Just like Charlie "Tremendous" Jones used to say, "You'll be the same five years from now except for two things: the people you meet and the books you read." Those two things can really alter your life's path.

People you meet can encourage you, and save you from a lot of problems by the things you can learn from their successes, mistakes and challenges. A book can change your life, too. I met someone yesterday who came to know God through reading a book. Before that, he didn't really claim to be a Christian, but he found this book in his barn and he didn't know who put it there or where it came from. It's interesting how those two things impact our lives so deeply in a good way.

When you see what your life's mission and purpose is, then you get out of your own way. I used to get in my own way, and sometimes I still do. I mean, I think that's what the Apostle Paul struggled with in the book of Romans:

> *"For what I am doing, I do not understand. For what I will to do, that I do not practice; but what I hate, that I do...O wretched man that I am! Who will deliver me from this body of death?"* (Romans 7:15, 24)

He goes on to talk further about that struggle with the flesh. When you learn to get out of your own way, life is a whole lot easier.

10

Call to Action

You can be a catalyst for good. Once you get off baby food, you should then be making hoagie sandwiches and feeding others. You know what I'm saying? Don't be a twenty-year-old Christian in the faith and still expect everyone to come and minister to you. You have got to grow up. You find true joy when you become an adult and start being of use to others. Then you become independent, even though in a way you're still dependent on everyone. This interdependence leads to connectedness, and that leads to joy.

I hope I've challenged you. Let me exhort you to go out and challenge others as well, by telling your own stories, reflecting on how this has come to reality in your own life, and encouraging others, because that is the greatest commission. That's discipleship. The salvation part is easy. This book is about discipleship and this is where everything falls apart. Salvation is only the beginning of the journey. The greatest commission is a process.

Someone told me that Ruth Graham's tombstone reads, "End of construction—thank you for your patience." Though you're not perfect yet, you're a lot further along than a lot of other people, so you need to be helping them earn their wings, so to speak. In aviation, when you "earn your wings" you're able to fly solo and also carry passengers, getting people to their final destination. That's a great metaphor for life.

I'll never forget my first solo flight, at the local airport in Carlisle, Pennsylvania, flying little single-engine Cessnas. I had this tremendous flight instructor who's still a very dear friend today. He sat beside me through all my flight instruction, so I would always think, "Okay, if I screw up, Captain's got this." (I always called him "Captain," because he was a pilot for United Airlines before retiring.)

Well, one day we landed, and he got out and said, "Okay, now I want you to go up and fly in that same pattern and land three times."

I was shocked. "By myself?"

"Yup."

I thought, "Wow, maybe I can do this."

One great thing in the pilot community is, after you land your first solo and get out of the plane, they tell you to pull your shirt out of your pants so they can "shirttail" you. They cut off the tail of your shirt and sign it. That's your rite of passage as flying solo.

The world is not centered around you anymore. Now, you're a servant. Now, you can go live a great life. The next step in training is doing solo cross-country flights, flying from one airport to another. You have to land and try to find someone around to sign your log book, just to prove that you landed there, and then fly to another airport, and then back to the first one. You fly to two airports and then back home, like a big triangle. Since you don't yet have your license, you can fly solo, you just can't take any passengers.

My wife had gotten me a teddy bear called Adventure Bear, with a red jacket, a silk scarf, and a leather cap with goggles. He would sit in the right-hand seat of the plane—my first passenger. I still have him. He was with me while I still had my training wheels, so to speak, while I developed my confidence in flying. (Believe it or not, I would talk to that bear when I was flying.)

Then you get your private pilot's license and start flying your friends and family around, amazing them (and yourself) at what you can do. When I passed my private pilot test, Captain said, "Congratulations, now you have your license to learn."

I'd just had a year and a half of training! What did he mean by "license to learn"?

He filled me in. "You're going to learn something from every flight. You're going to learn what you did right and what you did wrong. Just remember: it's not just controlling the plane—steering it, landing it, greasing the landing and all that stuff—everybody does that, and they think it makes them a good pilot. But what makes you a great pilot is good decision-making skills."

I'll never forget when I was doing some of that early training and I took off from Carlisle. Flying towards Gettysburg, I crossed over a mountain, when suddenly the ground disappeared because there was a blanket of fog and clouds below me. I couldn't see anything. Looking behind me, I could still see where I had come from. I looked ahead thinking, "I don't know where I'm going." (Early on in training, you don't fly by instrument, but by what they call pilotage—using a map, a chart, a ground reference to see where you're at.)

I realized I couldn't see "where I was at," so I quickly turned the plane around, landed back at Carlisle, and called the Captain to tell him I couldn't do my solo cross country that day.

"Why not?" he asked. I told him that when I crossed over the mountain, there was nothing but ground fog below and I couldn't see any reference point.

I'll never forget what he said: "You just made your first good decision. You would never have been able to land, so you came back. You know your limitations." Those are the things you learn when you fly.

Now, as an instrument-rated pilot flying for 18 years, bad weather is no problem; I just fly around it—they call it "threading the needle." There's a thunderstorm on my right and a thunderstorm on my left, so I fly through the hole between them, and there's a big rainbow behind it.

Looking back over my years as a pilot, I've learned a lot about life. Flying by instrument is like flying by God's Word. You don't look outside at the circumstances around you, you look at your instrument panel. That way you can weather life's storms, because you know your limitations. You become hungry and inquisitive, and you hone your judgment. You grow up so that you can teach others. And this, my friends, is setting a true course in your flight plans for life!

About the Author
By Emily Thoman

Gerry Wevodau has been a part of my entire life. While I haven't known him his whole life, I have had the privilege of riding as "co-pilot" through the stories of his past, experiences of his present, and visions of his future. I am Gerry's favorite daughter—his only daughter—and business partner.

My dad has always been one to take calculated risks—though, in his younger days, they may have been slightly *less* calculated! He grew up as one of four children in the farm country of Mechanicsburg, Pennsylvania. Days were spent with his brothers riding motorcycles and playing basketball; I'm sure I've even heard stories of shooting squirrels and tormenting cows.

My parents met when they were teenagers— he told us stories of being the stock boy in a grocery store who helped take the trash out for the deli girl, and being rewarded with a piece of pepper jack cheese. They were married at the young ages of 17 and 20 (yes, he went for an older woman!). Shortly afterward they had my older brother. Times weren't easy for a single-income family of three; my mom made everything she could herself (diapers, baby wipes, clothes, curtains, food made from scratch, etc.), while my dad worked hard to provide everything he could.

Before you knew it, there were two more kids in the house and the pressure was on my dad even more to provide. I've been told stories of the pressure and frustration he experienced as he entered into the insurance industry shortly after I was born in the late 1980s. My mother would harness the high school cheerleader in her and cheer my dad on through the tough times, making him chuckle along the way.

Since my dad lost his own father shortly after I was born, he leaned on his mentor Charlie "Tremendous" Jones to give him the tough love he needed to be a man and leader of his household. Charlie taught my dad many important life lessons, including "get on your knees and take your problems to God—no one else wants to hear your complaining."

In our growing up years, my dad instilled a sense of adventure into our lives, out of his own passion for life. I will never forget the time we went hiking at Ricketts Glenn State Park as a family, when I was about ten years old. There had been a lot of rain in recent weeks, which left many of the bridges on the trail washed away as the waters raged by. My dad calmly had his wife and three kids, ages eight to thirteen, crossing strong currents by shimmying over logs and stepping on rocks; in the middle of the strong current, my mother was in tears, worried for the safety of her babies!

When I was in high school, the four of us were flown by my dad to visit my older brother at a college out of state. I was the "co-pilot" with my dad when we ran into some very rough turbulence that was treating the small aircraft like a ping-pong ball. While my mother and younger brother proceeded to freak out, I stayed calm with my dad—if my pilot wasn't worried, neither was I!

I could go on and on about all the adventures my dad has taken and even included his children on. Within these stories there would be countless tales of my dad's character and how we overcame difficult circumstances and the challenges of life.

I have learned a lot from my dad, and continue to learn from him. He has always encouraged me to be self-sufficient, while reminding me of the importance of relying on God for help and never forgetting Him in times of success. He has been a prime example of how hard work can pay off and improve your life, even if it isn't exactly what you envisioned for yourself.

My dad has always been there for his family in triumph and trial. He has shown his daughter what to expect in a man as a husband and follower of Christ (and yes, I found a man like that!). As his business partner, I am learning every day what makes a great businessman (or woman) and how to have a successful business that stands apart from the rest.

If you would like to contact Gerry,
he can be reached at:

gerry@wevins.com

About Tyler's Light

Founded by Wayne Campbell after his son Tyler sadly passed away from heroin addiction as a result of taking opiates from having shoulder surgery. Wayne now travels and speaks to schools, churches and support groups, spreading the word about the dangers of opiate addiction and how you can speak up to help someone before it's too late.

If you would like more information about Tyler's Light or would like to schedule Wayne to come and speak you can reach him at:

www.TylersLight.com.